A C
for Reform

Fifty years of the IMF and World Bank

Oxfam Policy Department

A Case for Reform

Fifty Years of the IMF and World Bank

Oxfam Policy Department

Oxfam Publications

A catalogue record for this book is available from the British Library

ISBN 0 85598 301 9

Published by Oxfam (UK and Ireland)
274 Banbury Road, Oxford OX2 7DZ, UK
(registered as a charity, no. 202918)

Available in Ireland from: Oxfam in Ireland, 19 Clanwilliam Terrace, Dublin 2; tel. 01 661 8544.

Co-published with Community Aid Abroad, Oxfam America, Oxfam Canada, and Oxfam New Zealand. (Please see the back page for contact addresses.)

Designed and typeset by Oxfam Design, OX1622/PK/95
Printed by Oxfam Print Unit
on environment-friendly paper
Set in 10/12½ point Palatino with Franklin Gothic Book and Demi

Contents

A Case for Reform

This book is based on a briefing paper originally issued by Oxfam (UK and Ireland) in response to the World Bank report *Learning from the Past, Embracing the Future,* published in July 1994 to mark the fiftieth anniversary of the Bretton Woods conference.

Bretton Woods: the lost heritage

Fifty years ago, the Bretton Woods conference sought to build the foundations of a new world order on the wreckage of the old. President Roosevelt, in his address to the conference in 1944, challenged governments to prevent a recurrence of the 'great tragedy' of the 1920s and 1930s, when mass unemployment, financial instability, and trade break-downs increased international tensions and led to war. The system which emerged from Bretton Woods was flawed in some important respects, but the architects of the World Bank and the International Monetary Fund (IMF), which emerged from the 1944 conference, were inspired by a common vision and an ambition to address the great social and economic challenges of the post-war era.

Today, a similar vision is needed to address the challenges of the twenty-first century. Paramount among these challenges is that of ending the 'great tragedy' of our day — the tragedy which consigns one billion people in the developing world to poverty. As the World Bank assserted in its 1990 *World Development Report*, 'no task should command a higher priority for the world's policy makers than that of reducing global poverty'. Certainly, no subject commands a higher profile in the public statements of the World Bank itself. In 1992, the World Bank's President, Lewis Preston, declared:

Sustainable poverty reduction is the overarching objective of the World Bank. It is the benchmark by which our performance as a development institution will be measured.

Laudable as such commitments are, over the past fifty years the activities of the World Bank and the IMF have evolved in a way which is contrary to their founding objectives — and to the task of reducing poverty. The Bretton Woods system was created, with the experience of Germany in the inter-war period fresh in mind, to protect employment and regulate markets without recourse to extreme deflationary policies. Yet World Bank and IMF structural adjustment programmes, developed in response to the Third World debt crisis of the 1980s, have concentrated on achieving low inflation and deregulating markets to the exclusion of other considerations. The resulting deflationary pressures have undermined prospects for economic recovery. They have also contributed to high levels of unemployment and the erosion of social-welfare provisions for the poor. Meanwhile, market deregulation has brought few benefits for those excluded from markets by virtue of their poverty and lack of productive resources.

This is not to suggest either that the *objectives* of structural adjustment programmes, which are intended to establish budgetary stability and growth, are misplaced; or that there are painless alternatives. There is today a growing consensus that markets have a critical role to play in development, and that chronic budget deficits and balance of payments deficits must be addressed. It is also recognised that, in the creation of the crisis of the 1980s, the impact of external forces was compounded by internal factors, such as ill-conceived forms of State intervention.

What is clear, however, is that the policies of the Bretton Woods institutions do not sufficiently reflect the needs of the majority of the world's citizens. There is also a gap between positive policy statements and the reality of implementation. This gap is reflected in the World Bank's project operations. Guidelines for World Bank projects include far-reaching commitments to environmental protection and to the protection of local communities. In practice, however, these guidelines are all too often breached, and vulnerable communities suffer displacement from their homes, erosion of their land rights, and acute environmental problems as a result.

Embracing the future?

Against this background, the World Bank's long-awaited 'vision' document, *Learning from the Past, Embracing the Future,* published to mark the fiftieth anniversary of the Bretton Woods conference in July 1994, was a profound disappointment. Oxfam (UK and Ireland) had hoped that, in view of the failures of existing adjustment policies, the World Bank would accept the need for a wide-ranging policy review, with the full involvement of the relevant agencies of the UN and other representative interest groups. Such a review could have provided the foundations for a new development compact aimed at eradicating poverty. Instead, the 'vision' document reaffirms the World Bank's faith in existing policies, while tentatively acknowledging that a broader adjustment framework is necessary for sustainable growth and poverty reduction.

Similar problems arise in relation to the document's treatment of project lending. Despite a welcome commitment to 'increased awareness of and sensitivity to the social and ecological dimensions of development' in the Bank's project operations, any consideration of existing problems in implementing policy guidelines is conspicuous by its absence.

So, too, is any consideration of democracy in the management of the World Bank and IMF. While *Learning from the Past, Embracing the Future* rightly calls for increased accountability and transparency in the public sectors of developing countries, it does not apply the same principles to the Bretton Woods agencies themselves. This is a major weakness. The Bretton Woods institutions carry an immense responsibility, because the policies they advocate make a direct impact on the lives of millions of people in the developing world. Yet these policies are designed and implemented with scant regard for the principles of accountability and transparency which both the World Bank and the IMF advocate for developing countries. All too often, blueprints for structural adjustment are drawn up in Washington in accordance with the dictates of free-market ideology, and applied with insufficient regard to the circumstances of individual countries. Negotiations with governments are held in secret, and non-governmental organisations (NGOs) and citizens' groups are denied access to information. At the same time, information on World Bank projects often remains inaccessible and unreliable.

Oxfam believes that greater democracy and accountability on the part of Third World governments is vital if the challenge of reducing poverty is to be overcome. Without genuine democracy, the interests and aspirations of the poor will remain peripheral items on the political agenda. By the same token, however, democratisation should not be a one-way process. It is not acceptable for Northern governments to demand greater accountability on the part of governments in the South, when these same governments are effectively transferring economic policy sovereignty to remote, unaccountable institutions in Washington, controlled by the governments of the North. International good governance demands that developing countries be given a greater share of power in the World Bank and the IMF, through a reform of the current weighted voting system, in which a country's votes are determined by its financial contribution. It also requires that both institutions be opened up to greater public scrutiny. The Bank's recently established Inspection Panel, though a step in the right direction, will not achieve this objective.

Avoiding the challenge

The development objectives identified in *Learning from the Past* are very positive. Broad-based and shared economic growth, investment in health care and education, environmentally sustainable development, popular participation, and the empowerment of women are aims shared by Oxfam and many other NGOs. However, there is a gulf between these important principles and the reality which agencies like Oxfam confront in working to reduce poverty. In particular:

- Structural adjustment programmes are undermining prospects for recovery, compounding inequalities, undermining the position of women, and failing to protect poor people's access to health and education services.

- Project interventions funded by the Bank often continue to cause unacceptable — and sometimes violent — human displacement and environmental damage.

• Despite limited initiatives of a positive nature, there is no coherent debt-reduction strategy for the world's poorest countries.

• While endorsing 'good governance' in the South, the World Bank is itself unaccountable to citizens and governments in the developing world.

Learning from the Past has avoided addressing the real challenges facing the World Bank. The result is less of a 'vision' than a repackaging of received wisdoms, when the urgent need is for a fundamental review of World Bank-IMF policies and their implications for the reduction of poverty.

Structural adjustment programmes

The background

Structural adjustment programmes (SAPs), designed by the World Bank and the IMF, proliferated in the early 1980s, as one country after another in the South was afflicted by a lethal combination of high interest rates and falling commodity prices. Along with the loans from these multilateral agencies to cover balance-of-payments deficits and budget deficits came conditions. These required governments to comply with targets for reducing budget deficits, liberalising import restrictions, deregulating internal markets, and promoting exports. The stated objective has been to support export-led recovery. More recently, the World Bank and the IMF have asserted that SAPs constitute an integral part of a poverty-reduction strategy geared towards 'employment-intensive' growth.

Oxfam does not question the need for economic adjustment in developing countries that are facing chronic trade and financial problems. Nor is it suggested that there are ready-made painless alternatives available. However, World Bank-IMF adjustment programmes are deeply flawed in a number of respects, not least because they operate over an unrealistically short time-scale. For the world's poorest countries in particular, social and economic recovery from the deep crisis of the 1980s requires long-term planning for reconstruction. By contrast, structural adjustment has focused upon the attainment of short-term targets for reducing budget deficits and inflation. It is true, as the World Bank and the IMF claim, that external debt problems have intensified deflationary pressures. But the Bretton Woods agencies could have done far more to challenge the claims of creditors against the highly indebted countries of the South.

Instead, the IMF responded to the debt crisis by imposing a monetarist strait-jacket on much of the South, insisting upon punitive interest rates to meet targets for lowering inflation. Social-welfare provision and poor people's access to health care and education have been eroded by reductions in public expenditure. Moreover, potentially competitive labour-intensive industries and rural employment have been undermined by declining public investment in social and economic infrastructures, by credit shortages, and by foreign-exchange constraints. To make matters worse, the imposition of an 'export-led growth' strategy for resolving the debt crisis has carried the seeds of its own destruction, especially in the world's poorest countries. By expanding production of commodities such as coffee, cocoa, and tea for world markets which were already over-supplied, structural adjustment programmes contributed to the most protracted and deep depression in world markets since the 1930s (a structural trend which the mid-1994 boom in international coffee prices has not changed). Between 1979 and 1992, prices for beverages, which account for the bulk of Africa's exports, fell by three-quarters. The resulting deterioration in terms-of-trade, an index which measures the relative prices of exports and imports, cost non-oil exporters the equivalent of 5 per cent of their national income.

Against this background, any export-led strategy for growth based on primary commodities should have incorporated a wider strategy for regulating international supply and demand, at levels compatible with more remunerative prices. Further, it should have involved a more coherent approach to production, with adjustment policies being scrutinised to ensure that they were not fuelling over-supply and locking exporters into a downward price spiral. Instead, the World Bank's approach was to 'leave it to the market' — with disastrous consequences for low-income countries in particular.

It would be wrong to ascribe the worsening poverty in many developing countries entirely to World Bank-IMF policies. Inappropriate forms of State intervention, corruption, excessive military spending, and an adverse external trading and financial environment have all played a role in undermining human welfare. However, adjustment policies were a significant factor in consigning the world's poorest countries to a lost decade of economic recession and deteriorating human welfare in the 1980s. Today, the same policies are consigning the poor in wide swathes of the developing world to another lost decade of deepening poverty, rising inequality, slow growth, and mass unemployment.

The rich world can turn its back on the victims of these policies, but it will not escape the long-term consequences of failure to reduce poverty in the developing world. Mass migration, violent conflict, and the production by peasant farmers of commodities for the international narcotics trade are all symptoms of social and economic policy failure, in which structural adjustment continues to figure. The challenge of redesigning adjustment policies to meet the objective of poverty-reduction is a formidable one — as is the scale of the problem to be confronted in Latin America and Africa.

In **Latin America**, per capita incomes dropped by 10 per cent and investment fell from 23 per cent to 16 per cent of national income during the 1980s. Import activity dropped sharply, as governments transferred an enormous stream of wealth — totalling over $200bn, or some 6 per cent of GDP, during the decade — out of the region. Inevitably, deflation on this scale increased social misery, with the costs of adjustment passed disproportionately to the poor. The World Bank itself estimates that nearly 33 per cent of the region's population was living in poverty by 1990, up from 27 per cent a decade earlier; and an estimated 10 million children are suffering from malnutrition. Over the 1980s, the poorest 20 per cent of the region's population saw their share of income fall to less than 4 per cent. Unfortunately, as Oxfam pointed out in a report[1] issued at the time of the annual meeting of the World Bank and the IMF in Madrid in September 1994, the Bretton Woods agencies have remained oblivious to the connections between these trends and adjustment policies. The Inter-American Development Bank has identified inequality as one of the major obstacles to recovery in the region.

In **Africa**, where more than thirty countries have adopted structural adjustment measures, average incomes fell by 20 per cent during the 1980s, open unemployment quadrupled to 100 million, investment fell to levels which were lower than in 1970, and the region's share of world markets fell by half, to 2 per cent. Today, sub-Saharan Africa is the only developing region in which poverty is increasing and human welfare standards are worsening. Africa's recovery prospects have suffered acutely from the emphasis placed by SAPs on export-led recovery. As one country after another expanded production of primary commodities for stagnant world markets, they contributed to the worst international price slump since the 1930s. During the second half of the 1980s, for example, West African cocoa producers almost doubled their production, only to see their foreign-exchange earnings fall. The IMF now concedes that worsening terms of trade have undermined its adjustment programmes, and the World Bank's *Global Economic Prospects* report (1994) acknowledges that world prices for coffee, cocoa, and tea — Africa's major primary-commodity exports — have been depressed by over-supply.

Today, the World Bank and the IMF claim that their adjustment policies are working, and that sustained economic recovery is in sight. Oxfam is not convinced. In Latin America, where some countries are experiencing economic growth, there is little evidence to suggest that this recovery is being built on the foundations of domestic investment. Indeed, investment rates have yet to regain their 1980s value and are less than half the level of those in the high-growth economies of Asia. In countries such as Mexico, Brazil, and Argentina, stock-market booms, fuelled by privatisation, have been mistaken for stable recovery. The United Nations Conference on Trade and Development, most recently in its 1994 *Trade and Development Report*, has repeatedly warned of the dangers posed to social and economic recovery by unregulated financial markets — but to no avail. More significantly, economic growth has yet to translate into a reduction of poverty and inequality.

In Africa, claims that the World Bank's macro-economic reforms are yielding results are even less credible. The Bank's own most recent assessment of adjustment in the region, *Adjustment in Africa: Reform, Results and the Road Ahead,* confirmed that countries implementing SAPs were performing worse on investment and agricultural production than other countries. Earlier reviews by the World Bank and the IMF reached similar conclusions. This can be traced directly to the effects of IMF stabilisation policies on interest rates and public expenditure. The World Bank's own evidence confirms that there is little prospect of economic growth making an impression on poverty in the foreseeable future. In Ghana, the star pupil of both the World Bank and the IMF, the average citizen will not cross the poverty line for another half-century. Moreover, after a decade of adjustment and aid transfers equivalent to 8 per cent of national income, private investment in Ghana remains insufficient to replace existing capital stock, and the country's debt has tripled to over $4bn.

Employment

Contrary to claims by the World Bank and IMF that adjustment is creating a framework for labour-intensive growth and poverty reduction, Oxfam's experience suggests that SAPs offer a future of 'growth-through-exclusion', leaving the poor increasingly marooned among islands of prosperity. This trend can be traced in part to the pervasive influence of IMF stabilisation policies, which are geared towards lowering inflation to the exclusion of wider objectives such as generating jobs, reducing poverty, and promoting investment. The IMF's central policy instrument for reducing inflation is high real interest rates. However, these have been partly responsible for the disastrous failure of investment to recover under adjustment. Meanwhile, the World Bank's insistence on rapid import liberalisation has damaged the interests of the poor, by exposing labour-intensive industries, which are suffering from acute shortages of capital and foreign exchange, to a surge in foreign competition.

The result, in many countries, has been a process of de-industrialisation, and the collapse of potentially competitive industries. Inevitably, vulnerable communities have suffered form the resulting rise in unemployment. They have also been adversely affected by the deregulation of labour markets and erosion of minimum wages, which have reduced household incomes and left workers vulnerable to exploitation. The overall effect has been to transfer the costs of adjustment to low-income groups. Oxfam has witnessed the consequences across the wide range of countries in which it works:

In Zambia, fragile industries have been damaged by punitive interest rates and a surge in competition from cheap imports. More than three-quarters of Zambia's textile factories have closed in the past year, generating mass unemployment in urban centres. This has not prevented the IMF from lauding Zambia as a model to be followed by others for its achievements in lowering inflation.

In countries such as Mexico, Costa Rica, and Bolivia, average wages have fallen by one third since 1980 — and they are still falling. This partly explains the increase from 38 million to 69 million in the number of urban-based people living in poverty in the region. In Costa Rica, one of Latin America's model adjusters, the proportion of the population unable to meet its basic needs increased from 21 per cent to 28 per cent between 1987 and 1991.

According to the International Labour Organisation, real wages have fallen by between 50 per cent and 60 per cent since the early 1980s in most African countries. In Tanzania, by 1988 the average monthly wage was below the income level needed to buy enough food for an adequate family diet, and by 1991 it was insufficient to purchase twenty days' worth of food.

In Latin America, open unemployment has risen to an average of over 10 per cent, and is considerably higher in countries such as Peru and Bolivia. In sub-Saharan Africa, average unemployment in countries such as Zambia, Tanzania, and Ghana exceeds 20 per cent.

Rising unemployment and falling wages have been accompanied by a huge expansion of employment in the informal sector, which now accounts for around two-thirds of employment in Africa. This trend has been welcomed by the World Bank and the IMF as a move towards market 'flexibility'. However, that 'flexibility' entails the deepening impoverishment of women, who have been forced to take on multiple jobs, working long hours for low pay in the informal sector to maintain family incomes. The plight of poor women has been worsened by a steep decline in wages in the informal sector, which have fallen by almost 60 per cent in Latin America since the 1980s.

In Chile, widely cited as a model adjuster by the World Bank and the IMF, inequalities in incomes have widened dramatically, and low-wage, insecure employment is now the major cause of poverty. In 1990, minimum wages were 20 per cent lower than in 1980. Meanwhile, the income share of the poorest 20 per cent of the population fell by one fifth between 1980 and 1990. It is true that economic growth in Chile has significantly reduced open unemployment. However, in contrast to the situation fifteen years ago, when unemployment was the major cause of poverty, today two-thirds of the poor are in employment. However, around a third of those in work are in a precarious position, with no security of contract. Their poverty and vulnerability reflect the inherent limitations of a recovery strategy built on the foundations of low wages and 'flexible' labour markets — a euphemism for eroding the rights of workers. Oxfam has witnessed the effects of labour-market deregulation through its support for women textile workers in Santiago, many of whom are forced to work extremely long hours on a casual basis in order to survive. Unfortunately, both the World Bank and the IMF now regard the type of labour-market reforms introduced in Chile as a blueprint for all adjusting countries. The 1994 IMF *World Economic Outlook* advocated wholesale deregulation as a means of maximising employment. In Oxfam's view, this is a prescription for social dislocation and is inconsistent with the goals of reducing poverty and insecurity.

Trade union rights have been severely eroded in a number of adjusting countries. Chile under the regime of General Pinochet is the most extreme example. But the right to collective action in defence of wages has also been severely curtailed in Ghana, Zimbabwe, Mexico, and the Philippines.

In Latin America, adjustment policies have dramatically changed the profile of poverty in most countries. In addition to the general increase in poverty noted earlier, the number of people living in extreme poverty increased from 62 million to 93 million between 1980 and 1990. Over the same period, falling wages and rising unemployment increased the size of the urban poor population, which now accounts for 60 per cent of the total.

In the Philippines, the mass unemployment and impoverishment caused by stabilisation and structural adjustment forced destitute families to migrate from Manila to marginal upland forests and coastal areas to try to earn a bare subsistence, with devastating environmental consequences.

Oxfam has responded to the social pressures generated by structural adjustment through its overseas programme. That programme has supported self-help initiatives among urban populations in Africa, Asia, and Latin America who are seeking to defend their access to basic services and generate employment and income. However, programme interventions funded by external NGOs are not durable substitutes for macro-economic policy reforms. Adjustment policies must be redesigned to generate increased employment, notably through a relaxation of interest rates, selective protection, and carefully targeted State support for labour-intensive industries. At the same time, support for living wages and tolerable working conditions is vital to prevent the trend towards poverty in employment. There is little evidence to show that living wages and provisions to ensure secure employment undermine the creation of jobs, in either the developed or the developing world.

The rural sector

In the rural sector, the World Bank and the IMF claim that devaluation and the withdrawal of State marketing boards have reduced poverty among smallholder producers by increasing prices and reducing taxation. Given the background of over-valued currencies and the ruinous role of marketing boards in many countries, these are perfectly reasonable policy objectives. However, they do not amount to a coherent strategy for reducing poverty. Such a strategy must address the interlocking social, economic, and environmental pressures which consign poor people to a marginal existence.

Learning from the Past also ignores some of the critical issues of distribution which are central to pricing policies. Oxfam's experience is that, in the absence of redistributive reforms and effective State intervention in support of the poor, the benefits of increased prices tend to flow towards powerful traders and intermediaries. This confirms the broader lesson, which the World Bank and the IMF continue to ignore, that people operate in markets governed by power relations; and they leave the market-place with rewards which reflect those relations. The evidence across the developing world is that narrowly-defined reforms of pricing and marketing systems are an insufficient mechanism for reducing poverty.

In Ghana, research by the International Fund for Agricultural Development (IFAD) suggests that the benefits of pricing reforms have gone mainly to farmers producing cocoa for export, rather than to producers of staple food, who account for the majority of the country's poor. In Zimbabwe, tax and pricing reforms under adjustment have brought windfall gains for commercial farmers, but relatively modest improvements for smallholders.

In Zambia, Tanzania, and Mozambique, where Oxfam works with smallholder producers, higher prices have not 'trickled down' to the poor. Most poor producers are excluded from profitable trading by lack of land, credit facilities, and marketing infrastructure. Instead, the prime beneficiaries have been monopolistic private-sector traders, who are well placed to exploit the poorest producers and most marginal areas.

In the Sahel region of Africa, the liberalisation of agricultural marketing has had adverse consequences for many of the poorest producers. According to a World Bank technical working paper[2] on Senegal, Mali, and Niger, 'the withdrawal of parastatal agencies from the agricultural sector resulted in increases in farm-gate prices for inputs, due to the cessation of credit schemes. These increases in costs were not compensated for by increases in prices of crops and livestock.' The report goes on to note that low prices, along with the collapse of public investment in extension services, remain a major disincentive to increased investment.

Agricultural production is growing more slowly in sub-Saharan African countries which adhere most closely to World Bank-IMF adjustment policies than in other countries. According to the World Bank's paper *Adjustment in Africa: Reform, Results and the Road Ahead,* countries achieving the most substantial progress towards the macro-economic targets associated with structural adjustment achieve consistently lower agricultural growth-rates than those making more limited progress (or, for that matter, those making no progress at all). This finding has important implications for household food security. Independent research suggests that correlations between structural adjustment and lower agricultural growth-rates could be caused by the erosion of extension services (such as technical advice) and infrastructural support which results from cuts in public expenditure.[3]

In Nicaragua, Oxfam works with smallholder livestock farmers whose livelihoods have been undermined by restrictions on access to credit, following the introduction of an IMF stabilisation programme. As a result of tough new conditions and high interest rates, the amount of credit taken up by smallholders fell by two-thirds in the year following the introduction of the 1991 stabilisation programme. In Costa Rica, agricultural credit to small-scale farmers was cut by half during the second half of the 1980s, while the country's SAP diverted resources towards the commercial export sector.

In Zambia, the livelihoods of many poor farmers have deteriorated as a result of structural adjustment. As the World Bank itself has acknowledged in its recent poverty assessment for Zambia, smallholders across the country have been seriously affected by an IMF-imposed credit squeeze, which has reduced the availability of credit for production and marketing. Moreover, while prices for maize and other food staples have risen, the withdrawal of State marketing agencies has left poor farmers in marginal areas exposed to exploitation by powerful private-sector traders. In the Eastern Province, Oxfam's project partners have seen their household incomes fall, despite the increase in national maize prices, because of the low prices they receive from intermediaries. And in a recent survey of the position of small farmers in the Mumbwa District of the Central Province, Oxfam found that the poorest households, around half of which are headed by women, were trading on highly unfavourable terms. In August 1994, the Zambian Catholic Commission for Justice and Peace reported that poor farmers were bartering cereals for groceries 'at ridiculously low prices', and cited the exchange of a 15kg tin of maize for two tablets of soap, worth only a quarter of the value of the maize.

In Tanzania, Oxfam-supported groups in the Shinyanga region have been unable to market their cotton crop, because of the collapse of State-supported infrastructure and transport systems. As a result, producers have lost household income and the country has lost desperately-needed foreign exchange.

In the Philippines and the Andean countries of Latin America, import liberalisation has encouraged a sharp increase in imports of rice, corn, and other food staples. These imports have undermined the livelihoods of peasant producers and driven down rural wages and the household incomes of the poor.

In Mexico, adherence to IMF stabilisation guidelines in the 1980s resulted in a reduction of price support and credit

provision for smallholder maize farmers. This compounded rural poverty and encouraged more men to migrate to urban centres, adding to the labour burden of women. The future of the rain-fed, smallholder maize sector in Mexico remains uncertain in the face of moves towards trade liberalisation under the North American Free Trade Agreement. Some estimates suggest that as many as 6 million producers, mainly farming ecologically fragile hillsides, will be displaced by US maize exports.

Adjustment policies typically increase prices for commercial crops, where marketing is controlled by men, rather than improving prices for staple food crops, which are controlled by women. This has had important implications for the distribution of power and income within households. It also means that women have to work even harder to support cash-crop production.

What these cases illustrate is the danger of withdrawing State marketing arrangements, especially in the absence of a functioning private trading system. Whatever the past failures of government intervention in agriculture, the State has a vital role to play in developing agricultural production and food security. This includes acting as a buyer of last resort to maintain prices, providing credit and extension services to smallholder producers, and protecting local food systems from cheap imports. The State can also play a pivotal role in creating an enabling environment for smallholder producers. Oxfam's experience is that market interventions targeted at the poor — such as the provision of subsidised credit, other productive inputs, and irrigation — can improve both equity and efficiency. To put it another way, there is not always a trade-off between social justice and efficiency. This fact is underlined by the experience of Zimbabwe, where post-Independence investment in peasant agriculture resulted in sustained increases in production.

Social expenditure

The second central element of the World Bank's poverty-reduction strategy, alongside stabilisation and market liberalisation, is investment in 'social dimension' programmes, intended to protect the poor during periods of adjustment. In Oxfam's experience, some of these programmes have been relatively efficient in creating short-term employment opportunities for the poor, and in stimulating income transfers. The Bolivian Emergency Social Fund is one such programme. Other interventions have been less effective. All too often, social-welfare safety-nets have been created after the impact of adjustment has undermined the welfare of the poor. To make matters worse, most programmes are seriously under-funded. The Zimbabwe social fund for education, for example, would have been exhausted in 1992 if more than 5 per cent of the eligible population had applied for support. In addition, over-complex systems of administration have excluded many of the poorest people from social-welfare benefits, and in many cases the main beneficiaries have been civil servants, rather than unemployed formal-sector workers or rural smallholders.

But Oxfam's main criticism of the social provisions of adjustment programmes is that they offer a short-term response to a problem of long-term structural poverty. Simply 'bolting-on' social-welfare provisions to structural adjustment programmes does not amount to a strategy for reducing that poverty, especially when these programmes reinforce its underlying causes. What is needed is a more integrated approach, in which poverty-reduction is the focus and objective of macro-economic reform.

Learning from the Past gives considerable weight to social investment in health care and education, citing this as one of the keys to successful adjustment. This is a welcome commitment, which reflects the World Bank's efforts to improve its performance in supporting social-sector investment. World Bank spending in human-priority areas rose from 5 per cent in the early 1980s to around 17 per cent in 1994. But much remains to be done. In particular, the World Bank — along with other donors — must increase the proportion of social-sector support directed towards the very poor. In many countries, too much financial support is directed towards tertiary-sector spending on teaching hospitals and universities, rather than towards basic health care, primary education, and rural water and sanitation supplies, where benefits to the poor are maximised. Despite its public policy pronouncements, the World Bank also has a mixed record in protecting social spending during the adjustment process. In large measure this can be traced to the IMF's insistence on the attainment of unrealistic public-expenditure targets under its stabilisation programmes.

The World Bank's reviews of public expenditure provide an important mechanism for monitoring overall social-sector spending and its composition. However, these reviews have so far had a negligible influence on policy, which partly explains why governments can continue to cut priority-sector spending with impunity, even after making commitments to the contrary. In Oxfam's view, public expenditure reviews should be developed in partnership with UN agencies, governments, and citizens' groups to provide more effective protection of social spending, if necessary through mutually agreed conditions attached to structural adjustment operations. But it is not simply the overall *volume* of spending which is important. The Bank and the IMF have been strong advocates of 'cost recovery' in health and education. Translated into human terms, this has meant charging vulnerable people for services which should be regarded as a basic right. The predictable result has been a steady erosion of access, with women and young girls bearing the brunt of the cost.

Oxfam has welcomed the World Bank's commitment to protecting the interests of the poor through social investment. But, as in other areas, experience suggests that the will to translate that commitment into reality is lacking:

In the Philippines, real per capita spending on health was lower in 1992 than in 1982. Moreover, the share of health spending in the total budget fell from 3.4 per cent in the early 1980s to 2 per cent for the period 1990-1993. Meanwhile, the expansion of cost-recovery has undermined the access of the poor to health care.

In India, the Department of Rural Development cut its social-expenditure budget in the first year of the country's stabilisation

programme. This was followed in 1992-1993 by a 46 per cent cut in the rural sanitation budget and a 39 per cent cut in rural water-supply spending — areas of social expenditure which are vitally important in any programme aiming to reduce poverty.

In Nicaragua, per capita social spending is less than half the level of the early 1980s, following a significant decline in the late 1980s. Meanwhile, infant mortality rates are increasing, after declining steadily for more than a decade.

In Zambia, where the World Bank pledged to protect social expenditure, the 1992 education budget accounted for 9.1 per cent of the total budget, compared with 13.4 per cent in 1985. In the health sector, the World Bank has acknowledged that the introduction of user-fees is perceived by village women as a serious threat to their health, yet it initially supported their introduction. This picture is confirmed by Oxfam's project partners in Mumbwa, who cite high registration fees at health centres as a major reason for not taking children for treatment. These fees have had a detrimental impact on the provision of immunisation for measles, whooping cough, diphtheria, and tuberculosis — diseases which have re-emerged as major killers across the country.

In Zimbabwe, per capita spending on health care and education has fallen by one third since the introduction of an adjustment programme in 1990. This is despite a World Bank commitment to restore real spending in both areas to 1990 levels. At the same time, charges in the health sector were increased sharply, following advice from the World Bank and IMF. These charges have been directly responsible for a steep decline in attendance at primary health-care centres, and in the registration of women for ante-natal services. As an Oxfam report[4] shows, a direct connection can be found between increasing recourse to user-fees and worsening human-welfare indicators. It is encouraging to note that the World Bank has now withdrawn its support for user-fees in Zimbabwe.

Evidence from many developing countries has shown that economic pressures and the introduction of user-fees in education result in disproportionately higher drop-out rates among young girls.

Oxfam's experience across Africa, Asia, and Latin America is that the curtailment of social services has forced women to compensate by increasing their burden of unpaid work. Increased poverty, the collapse of water and sanitation services, and the erosion of primary health-care provision mean an increased incidence of poverty-related diseases — such as measles, cholera, and malaria — and oblige women to spend more time in caring for their families.

These facts call into question the World Bank's claim in *Learning from the Past* that its interventions have enhanced the welfare of the poor. True, governments in developing countries share significantly in the responsibility for adjustment policies which negatively affect the poor. Budgets for basic health care, primary education, and water and sanitation services are easy targets for governments seeking to meet budget targets prescribed by the World Bank and IMF. Meanwhile, subsidies for parastatals, military budgets, and spending on tertiary-level health care and education, where there are powerful domestic vested interests involved, are frequently protected from expenditure cuts. But, while the World Bank cannot be held responsible for the indifference of Third World governments to the plight of the poorest sections of their countries, it could do more to defend the interests of the poor.

The failure of the World Bank and IMF to protect social expenditure during adjustment is damaging on several counts. Above all, of course, it is damaging to the interests of the poor. It also threatens any prospect of sustained social and economic recovery. But it is scarcely less detrimental to the Bretton Woods agencies themselves, since it calls into question their wider credibility as institutions capable of addressing the challenge of reducing poverty.

Oxfam is concerned that the damage inflicted on today's generation by structural adjustment programmes will be compounded in the future. This is because of the important links between economic growth and poverty-reduction on the one side, and investment in health care and education on the other. Indeed, the World Bank itself has identified investment in primary education as the single most important determinant of the divergence in economic performance between south-east Asia and Africa. Yet partly as a result of its policies, primary-school enrolment in Africa has fallen from 80 per cent to 70 per cent since the early 1980s. With employment and international markets becoming increasingly knowledge-intensive, this is a prescription for long-term economic decline, rather than export-led growth.

Reforming adjustment

Oxfam believes that the current approach of the World Bank and IMF to structural adjustment is self-contradictory, and that it aggravates social injustice. It is contradictory because its focus on reducing budget deficits through public-expenditure cuts and high interest rates is undermining investment, employment, and any prospect of long-term growth. And it is socially unjust, because it is compounding already unacceptable levels of inequality. What is needed is a new approach to adjustment. That approach should do all of the following:

- **Emphasise equity in the adjustment process:** In 1990 the World Bank estimated[5] that an increase of 2 per cent in income tax on the richest fifth of the Brazilian population would generate sufficient resources to raise all the poor above the poverty line. There is a strong case for redistributive taxation on this scale. As a recent UNICEF report[6] has pointed out, personal income taxation in Latin America is only around half the average for all developing countries, even though average incomes are almost one third higher. Despite this, structural adjustment policies have relied on restricting public expenditure and increasing taxes on consumption (which fall most heavily on the poor) to meet targets for reducing budget deficits. Similarly regressive approaches to fiscal deficit-reduction have been adopted in Africa. In Zimbabwe, for example, taxes on the corporate sector, commercial farmers, and high-income groups have been reduced, to promote investment. Meanwhile, poor people have faced higher sales taxes and fees on health and education. What makes this approach doubly unacceptable is that the main beneficiaries of adjustment have been high-income groups. For example, tobacco farmers in Zimbabwe have received windfall gains from adjustment reforms which enable them to retain their export earnings in hard currency. These gains could have been taxed, in the interests of protecting the welfare of the poor. Commercial farm-land could also be taxed in the interests of efficiency as well as equity. Currently, over one third of that land, the most fertile in the country, is unused, because its owners treat it as a financial asset. Imposing a land tax would generate revenue which could be used for social-welfare purposes and to encourage the more productive use of farm-land.

• **Stress the importance of guaranteed access to a minimum level of resources, and the need for institutional reform:** Successful adjustment is not compatible with increased inequality. This is one of the lessons of the South-East Asian experience to which the World Bank and the IMF continue to turn a blind eye. Without effective taxation systems, minimum-wage legislation, agrarian reform, and social expenditure targeted on the poor, there is no prospect of SAPs creating a framework either for long-term growth or for poverty-reduction. The absence of land-reform from the adjustment agenda in Latin America is especially damaging, in view of the high degree of landlessness in the region. At the same time, public-sector reform is vital to the interests of the poor.

• **Protect potentially competitive labour-intensive industries:** The results of the World Bank's own research into the performance of the South-East Asian economies underline the importance of selective protection, carefully targeted subsidies for key industries, an expansionary economic environment, investment in infrastructure, and low real interest rates. Current practices in Africa, Asia, and Latin America ignore these lessons.

• **Withdraw user-fees for basic health care and primary education:** Oxfam's experience and the results of extensive academic research in Africa, Asia, and Latin America confirm that user-fees for basic health services undermine the welfare of poor people. Moreover, user-fees are a notoriously inefficient way of raising revenue. (In Africa, health fees seldom account for more than 5 per cent of the recurrent costs in the health budget.) The outcome is a system which minimises efficiency and maximises injustice. The alternative is for donors, UN agencies, and the Bretton Woods agencies to explore alternative, non-regressive revenue-raising measures, allied to financial support through, for example, debt-relief.

• **Protect and enhance social-welfare provisions through social conditionality:** The legitimacy of any sort of conditionality is open to debate. But it is clearly wrong to confine conditionality to the attainment of macro-economic targets, especially where these are likely to compromise the welfare of the poor. In Oxfam's view, social conditionality should be built into adjustment operations, with specific measures included to protect access to health care, education, and other social-welfare services, along with measures to target public investment on the poor. However, the introduction of social conditionality should go beyond a bilateral dialogue between governments and the World Bank-IMF, to include the relevant UN agencies and representative NGOs and citizens' groups. That dialogue should seek to establish measures for achieving tangible social-welfare targets, such as those agreed by the World Summit on Children. The World Bank's public-expenditure reviews, which monitor government spending, could provide a mechanism for tracking performance in this area. However, these reviews should move beyond a narrow focus on expenditure to consider the more important question of *access* to public services. There is little merit in governments increasing health spending, for example, if poor people are being excluded from services by user-charges. In this context, special attention should be paid to the problems faced by women in gaining access to health and education services.

- **Consider the implications of adjustment policies for women:** All too often, adjustment policies are designed with a disregard for their impact on women. The increasing casualisation of labour and decline in wages have had especially severe consequences for women, who are forced to work longer hours in adverse conditions to protect household incomes. At the same time, women are often excluded from markets by being denied access to credit and other productive resources. Unless these barriers are withdrawn, there is little prospect of women benefiting from market reforms.

World Bank projects: lessons unlearned

Learning from the Past concedes that 'the Bank Group has made its share of mistakes'. That admission is a welcome one, although it understates the social and environmental damage caused by some World Bank project lending. However, what matters more than the mistakes of the past is the Bank's apparent failure to learn from them. It is true that the Bank has adopted admirable social and environmental guidelines which address many of the concerns raised by Oxfam's project partners; but (admittedly without an overview of all project lending) Oxfam's experience suggests that, to date, these guidelines have done little to protect the interests of the communities affected by World Bank projects.

Oxfam's partners' experience and our analysis of specific projects funded by the World Bank suggests that local elites may have been the main beneficiaries of those projects, while the livelihoods of the poorest have been undermined, particularly through displacement. Women have suffered from the failure of project planners to consider the gender-related implications of their actions; and there has been a reluctance to share information. These 'problem projects' include the following:

• **The Sobradinho dam in Brazil:** This project displaced thousands of impoverished rural families, who lost their homes and livelihoods but were never compensated.

• **The Polonoroeste project in north-east Brazil:** In 1991, a World Bank report admitted that loans provided under the project to support landless labourers and small-scale producers were in fact monopolised by wealthier farmers. 'The bulk of the programme's three million low-income rural families, especially landless farmers, were excluded from credit and agricultural services,' the report concluded.

• **The Singrauli Super Thermal Power Plant, and associated open-cast coal mines in central India:** 23,000 people were forcibly displaced by this project. The loans have resulted in major problems for the Singrauli area: severe air pollution from coal and ash dust, which cause high rates of respiratory diseases; unemployment, particularly among the original local population; inadequate compensation for resettlement and rehabilitation; inadequate housing and the growth of slum settlements; and the pollution of drinking water.

• **The Carajas iron-ore project in Brazil:** Part-financed by the World Bank in 1982 with a loan of $305 million, this project was designed to spur economic growth in the eastern Amazon. However, the World Bank failed to make enough provision for the social and environmental impacts of the loan. As a result, the region has experienced the highest rates of deforestation, and associated environmental degradation, over the past two decades in the whole of Amazonia. As a consequence of the project, land values spiralled, leading to a boom in property speculation which resulted in thousands of peasant families and Indians being displaced from their lands, often violently.

• **Livestock schemes funded by the World Bank in Botswana:** The main beneficiaries of these loans have been a small elite of commercial farmers, many of them government officials; while the livelihoods of pastoral farmers have been jeopardised by ranches encroaching on communal lands. The schemes have contributed to over-grazing and desertification.

• **'Social forestry' projects supported by the Bank in West Africa, Peru, Colombia, and the Philippines:** These projects have encouraged timber exports, which in turn have contributed to deforestation and undermined the livelihoods of forest-dwelling communities. The financial benefits have gone to commercial companies.

Social tragedy has all too often been accompanied by apparent economic failure. According to the Wapenhans Report, which was submitted to the World Bank Board in 1992, one fifth of all projects were facing 'major problems' in producing a viable return on investment. Performance in Africa was especially poor, with a failure rate of over 50 per cent. In effect, these 'non-performing' projects added to the debt burden of host countries. If the costs of resource degradation and depletion, as well as the human consequences of displacement, were to be taken into account, the proportion of project failures would be considerably higher.

Social and environmental protection: rhetoric and reality

In response to public pressure, mounting with each new project fiasco, the World Bank introduced a comprehensive policy on resettlement in 1990. It was designed to protect the rights of displaced people, whose plight was dramatically highlighted by the case of the Narmada (Sardar Sarovar) dam project in India.

In 1992, the Morse Commission, set up to investigate problems with resettlement in the dam area, concluded: 'Involuntary resettlement resulting from the Sardar Sarovar Projects offends recognised norms of human rights'. The report went on to criticise plans to displace at least 100,000 people, many of whom are from tribal communities, in 245 villages, living in the area affected by submersion. It noted that the impact of canal systems, which would affect a further 140,000 farmers, had largely been ignored. But the most damning indictment was of the Bank's internal procedures. The report concluded that 'No adequate appraisals of resettlement and rehabilitation, or of environmental impact' had been made, and that the decision to proceed was taken 'on the basis of extremely limited understanding of both human and environmental impact, with inadequate plans in place and inadequate mitigative measures underway'. Morse went on to criticise World Bank staff in the India Department for deliberately misleading Executive Directors and Bank management in Washington on the scale of resettlement, and on problems over non-compliance with agreements. To our knowledge, none of the staff involved has been disciplined.

Other evidence suggests that this was more than an isolated example of mismanagement. Over the last seven years alone, World Bank projects have forcibly displaced 2.5 million people. Recently reviewing projects that had affected about 2 million people over the period 1986-1993, the World Bank admitted that virtually all them had failed to ensure that displaced people regained their former standard of living. Some of the problems were traced to slack project-preparation by Bank staff, and to lax management attitudes. Clearance was routinely given to projects that did not meet Bank safeguards; offending governments were not held to account; and little was done to remedy mistakes. But a deeper problem, which the report ignored, is the fact that these project failures have continued without an effective response from the Bank's Executive Directors, who have systematically failed to bring them to the attention of national legislatures.

The case of the Arun Dam in Nepal

The World Bank review of the resettlement of communities displaced by its projects acknowledges that 'the potential for violating people's individual and group rights makes compulsory relocation unlike any other project activity'. Yet it goes on to record serious underestimates of the numbers likely to be displaced. In India, where Bank guidelines were seldom applied, it admits that 'the overall record is poor to the extent of being unacceptable'. If the experience of one of the Bank's most recent big dam projects is an accurate litmus test of current practices, there is serious cause of concern.

Oxfam is concerned that a new project to construct a $770m dam in the remote and ecologically unique Arun valley in Nepal may repeat the bad practices of the past, and could produce irreversible damage. Relatively few of the tribal people living in the valley will have to be relocated. But Nepali NGOs are concerned that compensation rates for families losing land are set too low, and that families are being persuaded to accept cash instead of replacement land. If this is the case, many will be left destitute after a few years and forced to leave. Nepali NGOs also fear severe social dislocation caused by the building of roads and arrival of construction workers. With the opening of the road, forests will be accessible for illegal logging activities, which carry the threat of deforestation and soil erosion. This in turn will threaten the future viability of farming on the region's fragile hillside slopes.

For their part, Bank staff claim that the Arun Dam has an excellent environmental protection scheme — and they are pressing the Board of the Bank to approve the project. But it remains far from clear whether the Government of Nepal will be able to secure adequate finance. Moreover, Oxfam partners believe that the Bank has seriously exaggerated both the export and employment opportunities which the project will bring, raising questions about its economic viability. In addition, local markets will be disrupted by the influx of goods from outside. The Bank has admitted its failure to consider alternative schemes, such as small and medium-scale local private-sector projects, which would be better geared towards meeting local needs.

In mid-1994, many of the concerns raised by NGOs were echoed by the World Bank's Nepal Division Chief for Population and Human Resources, Marlin Varchus, who resigned because he had 'serious misgivings and reservations' about the Arun Project. In a public statement (9 September 1994), he explained that the scale of the project was liable to 'crowd out investments in the social sectors'. In his view, benefits would not readily trickle down to the poor, the overwhelming majority of whom live in rural areas that will not be served by the Arun project.

The case of Planaforo in Brazil

Oxfam is currently monitoring another unfolding disaster sponsored by the World Bank, this time in the Brazilian Amazon. The Rondonia Natural Resource Management Project (Planaforo) was approved hastily before the Earth Summit in Rio de Janeiro in 1992, despite warnings from NGOs that the State government of Rondonia had shown no commitment to enforcing its social and environmental provisions. These included, as a precondition for the World Bank loan, a commitment by the State government to halt illegal logging activities in Indian areas, and to stop encroachment into ecological reserves by land speculators.

Neither of these conditions was met. Oxfam warned that, unless the Bank took its own loan conditions seriously, Planaforo would only repeat the mistakes of the past. This is precisely what has happened.

Part of the rationale of Planaforo was to mitigate the effects of a previous integrated rural development project called Polonoroeste, costing $457 million. A major component of this project was the paving of a 1,500km road. The construction of that road accelerated migration into the largely untouched western Amazon, devastated Indian communities, and provoked large-scale, indiscriminate deforestation. The failure of the project's plans to protect Indian lands and the environment was subsequently attributed by the Bank to Brazil's 'inappropriate policy framework', weak institutions, and inadequate monitoring. Barber Conable, the Bank's then President, admitted in 1987 that Polonoroeste was 'a sobering example of an environmentally sound effort that went wrong'.

When the $167m Planaforo was unveiled at the Earth Summit, the Bank confidently asserted that 'the current project incorporates the lessons learned by both the government and the World Bank during the past decade about the necessary ingredients for sustainable development'. Yet three years after its approval, Planaforo seems set on the same disastrous course as its predecessor, with problems of non-compliance by the federal and State governments, and their official implementing agencies. The environmental protection agencies, despite receiving project funds, are not defending Indian areas and ecological reserves; the boundaries of many of the conservation units are being arbitrarily reduced; logging has intensified; and the State zoning regulations, which demarcate Indian lands and underpin the whole project, are being systematically violated.

The policy framework which undermined Polonoroeste has not been amended. Moreover, the government land agency continues to regard forest clearance as evidence of 'improvements', and on this basis awards definitive titles to land speculators. Peasant farmers, Indians, and rubber-tappers are suffering in the process.

Yet the Bank, although insisting that it cannot afford another failure in Rondonia, seems unable or unwilling to keep the project on course. The Bank has repeatedly stressed the importance of the participation of local NGOs in project decision-making, but in June 1994 the NGO Forum of Rondonia wrote to the Bank's President, Lewis Preston, calling for the project to be suspended. The Forum complained that NGOs' participation had been limited to superficial discussions of the annual work plans of the implementing agencies, that 'grass-roots proposals were not being incorporated', and that Bank missions had ignored NGO advice and, crucially, failed to address the discrepancy between government policies and the State zoning regulations. In August 1994, a Bank supervision mission, under a new project manager, visited Rondonia to review the NGO Forum's complaints. This resulted in an agreement that the Bank, the State government, and the NGOs would draw up a new management plan; that urgent studies would be undertaken in areas of land conflict; that guidelines would be drawn up clarifying land policies and procedures between the key State and federal agencies; and that measures to protect vulnerable isolated Indians and demarcate priority Indian areas would be taken. It is, of course, too early to judge what impact the new agreement will have on the implementation of Planaforo. What is clear, however, is that serious mistakes have occurred which could have been avoided. In view of the history of Polonoroeste, it was reckless of the Bank to press ahead with the project, without ensuring that adequate mechanisms were in place to implement and monitor the programme. Even under the new agreement, the Bank has failed to establish clearly identifiable benchmarks to measure progress, and the future of Planaforo still hangs in the balance.

The World Bank Inspection Panel

In September 1993, the World Bank established an Inspection Panel to investigate complaints from communities affected by its projects. The introduction of independent and effective scrutiny is welcome. Unfortunately, the Inspection Panel, as currently constituted, will be neither independent nor effective, for four reasons:

- The Executive Directors of the World Bank can arbitrarily block investigations into complaints.

- The Panel can only make recommendations. It cannot demand compliance or compensation, which will be determined by the Executive Directors.

- Procedures are ambiguous and do not specify whether complainants will be able to comment on the response of Bank staff to their complaints.

- Successful complaints will result only in corrective action by the Bank, rather than compensation for affected communities.

Improving project performance

In 1992, the Wapenhans report, an internal World Bank review of the reasons for poor project performance, made a number of radical recommendations for improving the quality of project management. Few of its recommendations have been adopted — and even fewer effectively implemented. For example, economists still dominate project design, implementation, and evaluation, even though Wapenhans called for social scientists to assume more responsibility in these areas. Similarly, while there have been tentative moves towards improved accountability, Bank staff are reluctant to act on Wapenhans' call for tough action to counter non-compliance. Calls for greater realism have also failed to end the presentation of unduly optimistic and misleading accounts of project performance to the Bank management, and the impetus to lend at any cost remains compelling.

More generally, in Oxfam's experience the World Bank's commitment to a 'bottom-up' approach to development has yet to be translated into action. In the cases presented here, it is ill-equipped to deal flexibly with smaller-scale projects and local NGOs. Oxfam's Brazilian project partners negotiating with the Bank for funds from the Pilot Programme for the Brazilian Rainforest, agreed at the Earth Summit, have complained about the Bank's protracted and unnecessarily complex procedures for appraising small demonstration projects.

But perhaps the deepest flaw in World Bank project lending is that identified by Wapenhans: namely, its failure to address the problem of non-compliance with the social and environmental guidelines established to protect local communities. In most cases, these are empty formulas, honoured more in the breach than in the observance. In Oxfam's view, this will remain the case until the Bank introduces effective cross-conditionality, in which all project lending is made conditional on compliance with social and environmental guidelines in every project.

Against this background, Oxfam believes that the World Bank must introduce major reforms into its project operation, including:

- remedial action for people affected by past projects: this should cover not just people displaced by large projects, but those whose way of life was severely disrupted by in-migration, through the Bank's support for road construction or colonisation projects;

- the cessation of loans for projects involving displacement, unless:

  ◆ the environmental and social implications of the project have been properly understood, considered, and approved by the affected communities;

  ◆ the affected communities have been given free access to the project's Environmental Impact Assessments (which, despite new World Bank guidelines, often remain undis-closed), and have been directly involved in drawing up the resettlement and rehabilitation plan, including mitigation plans to deal with adverse environmental effects;

  ◆ the affected communities understand and approve the criteria for paying compensation and settling disputes;

- finance for resettlement, rehabilitation, and environmental protection is secured *before* the project is approved;

- an independent panel has been set up to monitor compliance with the loan agreements, and to protect the rights of affected populations, with powers to halt disbursements and delay construction of infrastructure if necessary;

- national laws, guaranteeing the rights of displaced populations, are enacted and in force *before* the Bank proceeds with a project loan.

Participation and decentralisation

Learning from the Past states the World Bank's commitment 'to enhance the participation of the poor in the design and implementation of Bank-financed projects and programmes'. To date, its main activities in this area have involved support for decentralisation of political structures. In Oxfam's experience, decentralisation and participation can be useful instruments for supporting community involvement. But success depends critically on the prevailing local conditions and the development of genuinely consultative mechanisms for dialogue. All too often, these conditions are ignored.

The decentralisation model followed by the World Bank is the Mexican Municipal Funds Program (FMS), which it helped to design. This project, which is part of the National Solidarity Program in Mexico, has the aim of increasing the capacity of municipal governments to respond to development needs with greater efficiency and accountability. Although the FMS has achieved some successes in funding local projects among poor communities, it has been subject to political manipulation by Mexico's governing Institutional Revolutionary Party (PRI). The Bank's optimistic assessment of this strategy is not justified by the evidence. An internal report about the functioning of the FMS in the state of Oaxaca, prepared for a World Bank Workshop on participation, noted that:

Project selection under FMS did not necessarily prioritize the most pressing basic service needs. A large minority of FMS projects seemed to have little impact on poverty alleviation — despite the fact that the funds were to be spent on projects that 'benefit the largest number of least favoured residents'. In 1991, in Oaxaca, for example, over 25 per cent of the project funding went into the category called 'urbanization' — e.g. paving the town square, building park benches, etc.

Whatever the successes and shortcomings of the FMS, its transferability to other countries is very much open to question. For example, in Brazil the Bank has seen 'municipalisation' as a mechanism for addressing problems associated with its projects. The Planaforo project, discussed above, is a case in point. In this case, the World Bank has proposed transferring administrative responsibility from a State government, notorious for allegations of corruption and the protection of vested interests, to municipal bodies. The problem is that municipal bodies in the project area share many of the problems associated with State bodies. Similar problems have emerged with the Small Farmers Support Project in north-east Brazil. This project is administered by local authorities, many of which are dominated by landed interests and have proved unresponsive to the needs of small farmers and landless labourers. What these cases illustrate is that 'municipalisation' is all too often a euphemism for disempowering the poor in the interests of the wealthy.

This is not to deny the case for transferring decision-making towards accountable, local political structures. But while the benefits of locally-based participatory development are beyond dispute, real participation requires effective consultation with the communities affected, rather than the implementation of pre-designed blueprints, which have little regard for prevailing local circumstances. Unfortunately, the development of genuinely participative structures is hard to reconcile with the Bank's top-down approach to development, which remains firmly in place. Staff are still constrained by inflexible procedures governing procurement and disbursement; they are based mainly in Washington, and rarely develop a rapport with local organisations; they are unable to monitor effectively the performance of implementing agencies; and there are few real incentives for staff to carry out participatory work, given pressure to achieve lending targets. In short, the World Bank's practice is likely to continue falling short of its aspirations to become 'a listening bank'.

This was recently underlined by the Bank's response to reports from Oxfam project partners in Brazil of invasions of protected Indian areas and ecological reserves. These reports have been dismissed by Bank staff as 'unreliable' and left uninvestigated. As a result, large-scale logging and encroachment are continuing to destroy the livelihoods and resource-base of indigenous peoples and communities of rubber-tappers.

In Oxfam's view, fundamental reforms are needed to improve the World Bank's approach to participation. In particular:

- Decentralisation should be promoted only in municipalities where local government is genuinely accountable and the political climate for participation favourable. In developing policy, the Bank, which generally has little field presence itself, should attach more weight to the views and experience of representative local organisations.

- Local capacity-building is required to enable local communities and representative organisations to play an effective part in project-design, implementation, and monitoring.

- The Bank should adopt a 'process approach' to projects, in which objectives are developed in the light of experience, and it should be ready to accept changes proposed by local communities. At present, legal and political impediments hinder effective responses to problems.

Reducing the burden of debt

Learning from the Past is conspicuously silent on the issue of Third World debt. During the 1980s, the World Bank and, more especially, the IMF uncritically endorsed creditors' claims that debtor countries should honour their debts in full. From this it followed that the only proper solution to the debt crisis was to divert resources on a scale which would inevitably limit growth, and to impose enormous social costs — which is what happened. By 1988, net financial transfers to developing countries were running at *minus* $20bn per annum.

This perverse transfer of resources from the poor world to the rich should not have happened. Indeed, the IMF and the World Bank were created, in part, to moderate the extreme effects of unregulated cycles of financial markets, in the interests of smoothing out adjustment processes, and enabling countries to grow out of debt. John Maynard Keynes himself, one of the main architects of the Bretton Woods institutions, envisaged a tax on 'surplus' countries to ease the adjustment problems of 'deficit' countries. This could have been facilitated by reducing debts, which formed a part of the resolution of all previous debt crises. Instead, having accepted that the debt *should* be paid, the World Bank and the IMF imposed the deflationary conditions under which it *could* be paid, with little regard to the enormous social costs involved. In the case of Latin America, social expenditures were cut and domestic economies squeezed to facilitate the transfer of financial resources equivalent to five per cent of regional income. Many of the problems facing developing countries today can be traced back to this decision, taken in the early 1980s.

To make matters worse, the Bretton Woods institutions emerged as components of the debt problem for many countries. Between 1983 and 1987, net transfers to the IMF from developing countries amounted to *minus* $8bn, and transfers to the World Bank totalled *minus* $1.7bn. As the United Nations Development Programme report put it in 1992: 'The Bretton Woods institutions thus failed many developing countries at their time of greatest need.'

That failure has continued. The debt crisis has all but disappeared from the international agenda, following the debt-reduction measures introduced in 1989 under the Brady Plan, which has benefited the major Latin American debtors; but sub-Saharan Africa continues to stagger under a massive burden of debt. That burden represents over 100 per cent of the region's income, so that its citizens owe more than they earn. The people of Zambia and Tanzania owe their countries' external creditors around four times what they earn. Repeated rescheduling operations, in which repayments are deferred to a future date, do little more than obscure the fact of bankruptcy. Each year Africa is drained of more than $10bn in debt repayments to the North — more than four times the sum which the region spends on health care for its citizens. Even this represents only part of the problem, since it amounts to less than half of scheduled repayments, so that arrears are building up at a frightening rate.

Current debt-relief initiatives, including the Trinidad Terms, proposed by the British Government in 1990 and recently adopted by the Paris Club, to ease the burden of government-to-government debt owed by the poorest nations, will not restore African and other low-income countries to financial viability. This is partly because the debt-reduction element envisaged is too small, a point which the World Bank acknowledges. But another reason is the failure of Northern governments to address the problem of multilateral debt, which is a problem for more than 30 countries. The IMF continues to receive from developing countries around $4bn annually more than it provides in new resources; and World Bank transfers have also remained negative since 1989, although the agency remains the major source of concessional finance ('soft' loans) for sub-Saharan Africa. These trends reflect the increasing pressure of the IMF and the World Bank in the debt profile of developing countries.

Of particular concern in this context is the position of low-income countries, which have been by-passed by the increase in foreign investment into middle-income countries. Since 1982, the stock of multilateral debt owed by severely indebted low-income countries has quadrupled to over $40bn, and servicing that debt absorbs around one third of total payments. The IMF represents a special problem, since it has extracted over $2bn from Africa alone since the mid-1980s. In the extreme case of Uganda, repayments to the IMF now represent over half of national repayments — or $100m annually. Projected debt service for Nicaragua for 1994 was $238m, or 13 per cent of GDP — of which two-thirds will go to the World Bank and the IMF.

Oxfam believes it is time for the World Bank to spearhead an international initiative to address the debt crisis of the world's poorest countries. That initiative should include measures to reduce official debt on a more substantial scale than currently envisaged, together with measures to reduce multilateral debt. The latter is vital, to prevent the continued recycling of desperately needed development assistance to the World Bank and the IMF in the form of debt repayments. Against this background Oxfam has called for:

- **A comprehensive write-off of official debt owed by severely-indebted low-income countries to governments.** This should be in the range of 80 –100 per cent, and should apply to the total debt stock.

- **The writing off of IMF debt in severely indebted low-income countries, through a debt-reduction facility financed by a sale of gold stocks.** The British government's recent initiative in this area is a step in the right direction. Under its proposal presented to the Commonwealth Finance Ministers in September 1994, up to 10 per cent of the IMF's gold stocks would be sold over a period of years, with the proceeds invested in financial securities. The interest from these securities would be used to finance a reduction in debt repayments for low-income countries facing problems with multilateral creditors. Oxfam has reservations both about the capacity of the British proposal to generate resources on the scale required and about the country coverage. It also rejects the linkage, which the proposal does not question, between eligibility for debt relief and adherence to IMF stabilisation programmes. However, the British initiative is important, because it establishes the principle that multilateral debt problems can be addressed by generating additional resources within the international financial institutions themselves, rather than by diverting development assistance.

• **A new issue of Special Drawing Rights (SDRs) targeted at developing countries.** In effect, SDRs are an asset which the IMF can provide to its members, to exchange for hard currencies when they are facing shortages of foreign exchange. The IMF's managing director has been pushing for a new allocation of SDRs, amounting to over $52bn, partly to help finance the imports of middle-income developing countries, and partly to support reconstruction in eastern Europe and the former Soviet Union. Not surprisingly, this proposal enjoys the strong support of the more powerful developing countries and former communist countries.

In Oxfam's view, there is a strong case for the Group of Seven industrialised countries to agree to a new issue of SDRs, the last of which happened in 1981. The argument that this would be inflationary ignores the obvious fact that SDRs represent a minute proportion (less than 2 per cent) of global reserves, and that, properly allocated, they would enable countries to expand output and employment. However, the real issue is not so much the size of the IMF's SDRs, but their dispersal. Under current arrangements, each country's share of SDRs depends on the size of its economy, so that most are allocated to the big industrial economies which are least likely to use them. What is needed is a reallocation of SDRs towards poor countries with little access to capital markets. In this context, the use of SDRs to finance debt-reduction measures in severely-indebted low-income countries could play an important role in reducing the foreign-exchange constraints which are hampering their recovery.

• **The use of the World Bank's reserves (currently totalling over $17bn) to provide debt relief on a selective basis on non-concessional ('hard') debts owed to the International Bank for**

Reconstruction and Development. This would bring immediate benefits for countries such as Nicaragua, Bolivia, Honduras, Tanzania, and Kenya, which are seriously affected by their level of debt to the International Bank for Reconstruction and Development.

Many Northern governments continue to reject multilateral debt reduction as impractical. But the alternative is to allow the degeneration of the multilateral financial system. Currently, that system is having to provide increasing amounts of finance simply in order to service past debts, rather than to finance development. In 1992, multilateral development banks (excluding the IMF) made lending commitments of $50bn to all developing countries, to achieve net transfers of only $4.6bn. The net disbursements of the International Bank for Reconstruction and Development, the commercial loan arm of the World Bank, were a mere $2.3bn in 1992-93 and minus $0.7bn in 1993-94. Even soft loans from the International Development Association were projected to total only around $5bn in 1993-94. This is incompatible with the task of providing long-term development finance on the scale needed.

Reforming the system

The fiftieth anniversaries of the Bretton Woods conference and the signing of the UN charter provide an opportunity for the international community to reflect on the kind of world we all want to see in the next century. What is needed is a wide-ranging debate on the failures of the past and the challenges of the future, rather than a justification of the present, such as is offered by *Learning from the Past*.

To date, the debate about the future has been dominated by the concerns of Northern governments over global currency instability. The Naples summit of the Group of Seven industrial countries in 1994 broadly endorsed the recommendation of the Bretton Woods Commission, chaired by Paul Volcker,[7] that the IMF be given responsibility for managing floating exchange-rates. This would restore to the Fund a role it lost with the collapse of fixed exchange-rates in the early 1970s. Potentially, it would also bring some order to an international monetary system in which speculative activity threatens to destabilise the whole world economy. Implementation of the long-standing proposal to levy a tax on foreign-exchange transactions would help to facilitate effective currency management. That tax could be usefully deployed in supporting sustainable development initiatives in the South, notably by financing the attainment of the central objectives agreed at the Earth Summit in Rio in 1992.

Other reforms advocated by the Bretton Woods Commission, and broadly endorsed by the British government, are more questionable. For example, the proposal to expand the proportion of World Bank resources directed towards the promotion of private-sector investment could divert concessional development finance away from the poorest countries. It also overlooks the vital role of the public sector in restoring social and economic infrastructure, even in countries currently attracting substantial foreign capital. Contrary to prevailing orthodoxies in the World

Bank, there remain many areas of public-service provision which the private sector is ill-equipped to offer, except to higher-income groups able to pay commercial rates.

But Oxfam's concern with the Bretton Woods report is not only with its tendency to treat privatisation as a universal panacea, but also with its more fundamental failure to examine the impact of World Bank-IMF policies on global poverty. That failing is reflected also in the wider debate on the future of the Bretton Woods system, much of which has ignored issues of concern to the South. This is unacceptable, both because of the overwhelming importance of addressing the challenge of reducing global poverty; and because of the critical role of the World Bank and the IMF in North-South dialogue.

In addition to the reforms discussed earlier, Oxfam believes there should be a five-point agenda for restructuring the Bretton Woods system:

• **First, the Bretton Woods system must be opened to wider public scrutiny, and be made more accountable.** It is unacceptable for Northern governments to demand, in the name of 'good governance', greater democracy and accountability on the part of Southern governments, when these same governments are effectively transferring sovereignty over policy matters to the IMF and the World Bank. In this context, the proportion of votes allocated to countries on the basis of their financial contribution to the World Bank and the IMF should be reduced, and a more democratic voting structure developed. At the same time, the development of civil society in the South would be enhanced by greater openness and transparency. As a starting point:

- The IMF should be required to publish its Letters of Intent — in effect,a contract setting out the conditions for its loans to governments — before the conclusion of an agreement. This would facilitate public debate and give citizens' groups an opportunity to influence critical decisions about public spending.

◆ The World Bank should be required to publish its policy recommendations at a similarly early stage in adjustment negotiations. In the case of projects, virtually all documents should be released during early planning phases. The Bank should ensure that a wide range of environmental and social documents, already theoretically available under the Bank's revised information policy, are genuinely made available in borrower countries. The Inspection Panel created in 1993 is unduly restricted in its actions and sphere of competence, and it is seriously under-funded. This is in stark contrast to the panel created to investigate complaints about the Narmada dam in India, which was highly critical of the Bank. Major reforms are therefore needed to make the existing panel a similarly effective body for examining complaints from citizens' groups.

◆ Executive Directors of the World Bank and IMF should be required to declare in advance to national legislatures their voting intentions on projects and adjustment programmes. They should also be required to report regularly to national legislatures. By extending public scrutiny, this would make it more difficult for Executive Directors to act, as they do at present, simply to legitimise pre-determined World Bank policies.

• **Second, the policy-making role of the IMF in developing countries should be ended, and its lending programmes halted.** These programmes are too short-term, insufficiently concessional, and governed by unduly restrictive conditions to contribute to the type of long-term recovery planning that is needed in most developing countries. In Oxfam's experience, the Fund continues to be dominated by a narrow monetarist perspective, which attaches overwhelming weight to reducing inflation, at the expense of wider objectives such as reducing poverty and creating employment. Moreover, its failure to provide appropriate long-term concessional finance has left it in the invidious position of extracting finance from the world's poorest countries. Against this background, Oxfam believes that Northern governments should refuse to replenish the Enhanced

Structural Adjustment Facility, through which the IMF provides concessional loans to the world's poorest countries, and transfer resources to a more appropriate body. They should also, as a matter of urgency, break the link between debt-relief measures and compliance with IMF programmes.

• **Third, the industrial countries should agree to a new allocation of Special Drawing Rights (SDRs), as proposed by the Fund's Executive Director.** Given the depressed state of the world economy, this would be unlikely to generate inflationary pressures, and it would help to boost growth. However, the distribution of SDRs should be weighted heavily in favour of developing countries, especially severely indebted low-income countries. Without such an allocation, shortages of foreign exchange in these countries will force them to depress domestic demand, with inevitable consequences for human welfare, and limit the imports needed to accelerate recovery.

• **Fourth, the Bretton Woods agencies should be integrated more effectively into the UN system.** Specialised agencies within that system should assume a far greater policy-making role in the design and implementation of adjustment policies. More immediately, the UN's expert Committee on Economic, Social and Cultural Rights should assume responsibility for scrutinising structural adjustment programmes, and monitoring their impact on the human rights set out in the International Covenant on Economic, Social and Cultural Rights. The IMF and the World Bank should also be made directly accountable to the UN Commission for Sustainable Development, which should demand more effective and transparent evaluations of the impact of structural adjustment, and project lending, on the environment.

• **Fifth, current approaches to adjustment should be reformed.** The World Bank should accept the legitimacy of a far wider range of adjustment reforms than are currently incorporated in structural adjustment programmes. Stated differently, an acknowledgement of diversity should replace the free-market monotheism which dictates current adjustment programmes. In this context, there is an urgent need to involve specialised UN agencies, representative citizens' groups, and governments in a genuine dialogue over adjustment. That dialogue should focus on developing expansionary policies, designed to maximise employment and eradicate poverty. State provision of marketing and infrastructural support to smallholder producers, selective and carefully targeted protection for labour-intensive industries, and redistributive fiscal and land policies all have a critical role to play. The World Bank should also establish specific and binding targets for improving poor people's access to social services. Progress towards these targets should be closely monitored, and well-founded complaints investigated by appropriate UN bodies such the Committee of Economic, Social and Cultural Rights. In brief, what is needed is an acceptance of greater diversity in economic reform, allied to more rigorous protection of social-sector provision.

Conclusion

Half a century on from the establishment of the Bretton Woods institutions, now is the time for a fundamental reappraisal of the roles and policies of the World Bank and IMF and their impact on the world's poor. These institutions, which were created to enhance global prosperity, exercise a powerful influence on the lives of poor people in the South. Yet both agencies are remote from the poor, and remain firmly under the control of Northern governments.

It is clear that the policy prescriptions of the IMF and World Bank do not sufficiently reflect the needs of the poor majority in the developing world. As the evidence presented here shows, structural adjustment programmes and some of the projects funded by the World Bank are at best failing to tackle poverty, and at worst compounding problems rooted in poverty and injustice. Moreover, political will is still lacking to pursue a credible debt-reduction strategy to ease the pressures on the most severely indebted low-income countries.

It is encouraging that inside the World Bank increasing emphasis is being placed on the over-riding importance of reducing global poverty, and (in some quarters) on the need to engage in meaningful dialogue about policy with NGOs and citizens' organisations. Yet there are stark contrasts between the Bank's positive statements of intent and the daily reality, experienced by Oxfam staff and partners, of the impact of current policy prescriptions on the poor. On the evidence of these contrasts, there is a compelling case for reform.

Notes

1 'Structural Adjustment and Inequality in Latin America: How IMF and World Bank Policies Have Failed the Poor', Oxford: Policy Department, Oxfam (UK and Ireland), September 1994.

2 M. Speirs and O. Olsen: *Indigenous Integrated Farming Systems in the Sahel*, World Bank Technical Paper no. 179.

3 Paul Mosely: 'Decomposing the Effects of Structural Adjustment: the Case of sub-Saharan Africa', University of Reading, 1993; Jane Harrigan and Paul Mosely: 'Evaluating the impact of World Bank structural adjustment lending', *Journal of Development Studies*, Vol. 27, No. 3.

4 Jean Lennock: *Paying for Health: Poverty and Structural Adjustment in Zimbabwe*, Oxford: Oxfam (UK and Ireland), 1994.

5 UNICEF: *Poverty and Inequality in Latin America*, 1993.

6 Ricardo Carciofi and Oscar Cetrangolo: *Tax Reforms and Equity in Latin America: a Review of the 1980s and Proposals for the 1990s*, Florence, UNICEF, 1994.

7 Bretton Woods Commission, *Bretton Woods: Looking to the Future*, Washington, July 1994.

Further reading

Bretton Woods Commission, *Bretton Woods: Looking to the Future*, Washington, July 1994

Carciofi, R. and O. Cetrangolo, *Tax Reforms and Equity in Latin America: A Review of the 1980s and Proposals for the 1990s*, Florence: UNICEF, 1994

Cornia, G., 'Is adjustment conducive to long-term development? The case of Africa', in Cornia *et al.*: *Africa's Recovery in the 1980s*, Florence: UNICEF, 1991

Cornia, G., *Macroeconomic Policy, Poverty Alleviation, and Long-Term Development: Latin America in the 1990s*, Florence: UNICEF, 1994

Diaz, A., *Restructuring and the New Working Classes in Chile*, Geneva: UN Research Institute for Social Development, 1993

Gibbon, P., *A Blighted Harvest: The World Bank and African Agriculture in the 1980s*, London: James Currey, 1994

The Ecologist, *World Bank Briefing*, Dorset: *The Ecologist*, 1994

The Guardian, *The IMF and the World Bank: The Next Fifty Years*, London: *The Guardian*, 1994

Lennock, J., *Paying For Health: Poverty and Structural Adjustment in Zimbabwe*, Oxford: Oxfam (UK and Ireland), 1994

Madely, J., *When Aid Is No Help*, London: Intermediate Technology, 1994

Mengisteab, K., 'Africa's debt crisis: are structural adjustment programmes relevant?', *Africa Development*, Vol. XVI, No. 1, 1991

Morse, B. and T. Berger, *The Report of the Independent Review of the Sardar Sarovar Project*, Ottawa, Resource Futures International Inc, 1992

Oxfam Policy Department, *Africa: Make or Break Report*, Oxford: Oxfam (UK and Ireland), 1993

Oxfam Policy Department, 'Debt Relief for Africa: An Oxfam Perspective', Oxford: Oxfam (UK and Ireland), 1994

Oxfam Policy Department, 'Structural Adjustment and Inequality in Latin America: How IMF and World Bank

Policies Have Failed the Poor', Oxford: Oxfam (UK and Ireland), September 1994

Rich, B., *Mortgaging the Earth: The World Bank, Environmental Impoverishment and the Crisis of Development*, **Boston, MA: Beacon Press, 1994**

Oxfam Policy Department, 'Structural Adjustment in India: Issues and Implications', Oxford: Oxfam (UK and Ireland), 1994

Rodrik, D., 'How should structural adjustment programmes be designed?', *World Development*, Vol. 18, 1990

Stewart, F., 'The many faces of adjustment', *World Development* Vol. 19, No. 12, 1991

UN Development Programme, *Human Development Report*, New York: United Nations, 1993

Watkins, K., *Multilateral Debt: The Case of Uganda*, Oxfam Briefing Paper No. 7, Oxford: Oxfam (UK and Ireland), 1994

World Bank, *World Development Report 1990*, Washington: World Bank, 1991

World Bank, *Effective Implementation: Key to Development Impact*, Report of the World Bank's Portfolio Management Task Force, Washington: World Bank, 1992 (known as 'the Wapenhams Report'

World Bank, *Implementing the World Bank's Strategy to Reduce Poverty*, Washington: World Bank, 1992

World Bank, *Poverty and Inequality in Latin America*, Washington: World Bank, 1993

World Bank, *Adjustment in Africa: Reform Results and the Road Ahead*, Washington: World Bank, 1994

World Bank, *Global Economic Prospects*, Washington: World Bank, 1994

World Bank, *Learning from the Past, Embracing the Future*, Washington: World Bank, 1994

World Bank, *Resettlement and Development: A Review of Projects Involving Involuntary Resettlement 1986-1993*, Washington, World Bank, 1994

Zattler, J., 'Adjusting adjustment', *Intereconomics*, December 1993

Other books in the Oxfam Insight series

The **Insight** series offers concise and accessible analysis of issues that are of current concern to the international community.

Paying for Health

Poverty and Structural Adjustment in Zimbabwe

Jean Lennock

ISBN 0 85598 293 4, 40 pages, August 1994

Jean Lennock shows how the most vulnerable sections of society carry the burden of structural adjustment when a government adopts the World Bank's advice to introduce user–fees for health care

NAFTA:

Poverty and Free Trade in Mexico

Belinda Coote

ISBN 0 85598 302 7, 56 pages, January 1995

Belinda Coote examines the impact of the North American Free Trade Agreement, which in 1994 created the largest free-trade zone in the world, and the first to unite countries from the developed and developing worlds. Will it lead to prosperity for all in Mexico, or will it leave the country open to exploitation and unfair competition? What are the lessons to be learned by other poor nations experimenting with policies of economic liberalisation?

Rwanda:

An Agenda for International Action

Guy Vassall-Adams

ISBN 0 85598 299 3, 72 pages, October 1994

Guy Vassall-Adams investigates the background to the genocide and refugee crisis which devastated Rwanda in 1994, and explores the reasons why the international community intervened too late to prevent the tragedy. The book argues for radical reform and proper funding of the UN's peacekeeping and emergency capacities, and presents specific recommendations for action.

Oxfam (UK and Ireland) publishes a wide range of books, manuals, and resource materials for specialist, academic, and general readers. For a free catalogue, please write to Oxfam Publishing, Oxfam House, 274 Banbury Road, Oxford, OX2 7DZ, UK.

Insight books are produced by Oxfam UK and Ireland as part of its advocacy programme on behalf of poor communities. They are co-published with other members of the international Oxfam group. For more information, contact your National Oxfam:

Oxfam America
25 West Street
Boston MA 0211 1206
USA
Tel: 1 617 482 1211
Fax: 1 617 728 2594

Oxfam Canada
Suite 300
294 Albert Street
Ottawa, Ontario K1P 6E6
Canada
Tel: 1 613 237 5236
Fax: 1 613 237 0524

Community Aid Abroad
156 George Street
Fitzroy
Victoria
Australia
Tel: 61 3 289 9444
Fax: 61 3 419 5318

Oxfam New Zealand
Room 101, La Gonda House
203 Karangahape Road
Auckland, New Zealand
Tel: 64 9 358 1480
Fax: 64 9 358 1481

Oxfam Hong Kong
Ground Floor 3B
June Garden
28 Tung Chau Street
Tai Kok Tsui
Kowloon, Hong Kong
Tel: 852 3 916305
Fax: 852 789 9545

The international Oxfams are autonomous, non-profit development agencies. They work to overcome poverty and social injustice through the empowerment of partner organ-isations and communities to achieve sustainable development and livelihoods, and to strengthen civil society in any part of the world, irrespective of nationality, race, political system, religion, or colour. They are Oxfam America, Oxfam Belgique/Belgie, Oxfam Canada, Community Aid Abroad (in Australia), Oxfam Hong Kong, NOVIB (in the Netherlands), Oxfam Quebec, and Oxfam United Kingdom and Ireland. The name Oxfam comes from the OXford Committee for FAMine relief, founded in Oxford, England in 1942.

Insight books are available through book distributors acting on behalf of Oxfam UK and Ireland.